Bipolar Disorder

Comprehensive Insights, Effective relief Strategies, and Coping Mechanisms for Managing Mood Swings and Enhancing Mental Health

Graham Julian Oliver

Disclaimer

The information contained in this book is intended for informational and educational purposes only and is not intended as a substitute for professional medical advice, diagnosis, or treatment. Always seek the advice of your physician or other qualified health provider with any questions you may have regarding a medical condition, including bipolar disorder. Never disregard professional medical advice or delay in seeking it because of something you have read in this book.

The author and publisher of this book make no representations or warranties about the accuracy, reliability, or completeness of the information contained herein. The strategies, techniques, and suggestions provided in this book are not guaranteed to work for every individual, and results may vary. The author does not assume any responsibility for any consequences arising from the use of this information.

Additionally, the author disclaims any endorsements with any individual, product, website, organization, or other names that may be referenced or mentioned in this book. Any such references are for informational purposes only and do not imply any endorsement or recommendation.

By reading this book, you acknowledge and agree to these terms and accept full responsibility for your decisions and actions.

Table of Contents

Introduction

Definition of Bipolar Disorder and Its Types (I, II, Cyclothymic)

Bipolar disorder is a mental health condition characterized by significant mood swings, including emotional highs (mania or hypomania) and lows (depression). There are three main types of bipolar disorder: Bipolar I, marked by manic episodes lasting at least seven days or severe enough to require hospitalization; Bipolar II, which involves a pattern of depressive episodes and hypomanic episodes but never a full manic episode; and Cyclothymic Disorder, featuring periods of hypomania and depressive symptoms lasting for at least two years in adults. Understanding these distinctions is crucial for accurate diagnosis and treatment.

To manage bipolar disorder effectively, it is essential to recognize the symptoms associated with each type. For example, individuals with Bipolar I may experience severe mood fluctuations that disrupt daily life, while those with Bipolar II might struggle with prolonged depressive states. Keeping a mood journal can help identify patterns in mood changes, aiding both individuals and healthcare providers in tailoring an effective treatment plan.

Importance of Awareness and Education for Effective Management

Raising awareness and educating oneself about bipolar disorder is fundamental for effective management. Understanding the symptoms, triggers, and treatment options empowers individuals to take an active role in their mental health. Education helps reduce stigma, fosters empathy, and encourages open conversations about mental health challenges, creating a supportive environment for those affected by bipolar disorder.

In practical terms, individuals can seek resources from mental health organizations, attend support groups, and engage in workshops that focus on bipolar disorder. Additionally, sharing knowledge with family and friends can create a stronger support system, helping loved ones understand the condition and how to provide appropriate assistance during mood episodes.

Importance of Early Intervention

Recognizing the Signs and Symptoms for Timely Diagnosis

Understanding the signs and symptoms of bipolar disorder is crucial for early diagnosis and effective management. Key indicators include extreme mood swings, ranging from manic episodes characterized by heightened energy, irritability, and impulsivity to depressive phases marked by sadness, fatigue, and hopelessness. Keeping a mood diary can help individuals track their emotions and behaviors, providing valuable insights that can facilitate a professional assessment.

Recognizing changes in sleep patterns, energy levels, and social interactions can also be instrumental in identifying bipolar disorder. It's important to observe not only your own behavior but also feedback from friends and family. If these symptoms persist for a significant period, seeking help from a mental health professional is essential for an accurate diagnosis and the development of an effective treatment plan.

Role of Support Systems in Managing the Condition

A strong support system plays a vital role in managing bipolar disorder effectively. This network can include family members, friends, and mental health professionals who provide emotional support, understanding, and encouragement. Open communication with loved ones about your condition can foster a supportive environment, making it easier to express feelings and seek help when needed.

Engaging in support groups or therapy sessions can further enhance your coping strategies. These settings provide opportunities to share experiences with others facing similar challenges, fostering a sense of community and reducing feelings of isolation. Learning from others' experiences can also offer practical tips for managing symptoms and navigating daily life more effectively.

Effective Medication Strategies

Medication is often a key component in managing bipolar disorder and can significantly stabilize mood swings. Commonly prescribed medications include mood stabilizers, antipsychotics, and antidepressants, tailored to individual needs. It's essential to work closely with a psychiatrist to determine the most effective medication regimen and to monitor side effects or any potential adjustments needed.

To ensure medication efficacy, maintain consistent communication with your healthcare provider. Keeping a medication journal can help track dosages, side effects, and mood changes, allowing for informed discussions during appointments. Adherence to the prescribed regimen is critical, as irregular use can lead to relapse or worsening symptoms.

Therapeutic Approaches for Mood Management

Therapeutic interventions, such as cognitive-behavioral therapy (CBT), can provide practical strategies for managing bipolar disorder. CBT focuses on identifying and altering negative thought patterns and behaviors, empowering individuals to cope with mood fluctuations. By setting realistic goals and learning problem-solving skills, individuals can enhance their emotional resilience and gain control over their mood swings.

In addition to CBT, incorporating mindfulness techniques can be beneficial. Practices like meditation, deep breathing exercises, and yoga help individuals stay grounded and focused, reducing anxiety and stress. These therapeutic approaches, combined with professional guidance, can create a holistic treatment plan that supports mental health and stability.

Lifestyle Modifications for Stability

Making specific lifestyle changes can significantly impact the management of bipolar disorder. Regular exercise, balanced nutrition, and sufficient sleep are foundational elements for mental well-being. Engaging in physical activities, even if it's a daily walk, can enhance mood and reduce anxiety levels. Establishing a consistent sleep routine helps regulate your body's natural rhythm, minimizing the risk of manic or depressive episodes.

Additionally, avoiding substances such as alcohol and recreational drugs is crucial. These can interfere with mood stability and exacerbate symptoms. Implementing healthy routines, such as meal prepping and scheduling exercise, can create a structured environment conducive to emotional balance.

Coping Mechanisms for Managing Mood Swings

Developing effective coping mechanisms is essential for managing mood swings associated with bipolar disorder. Techniques such as journaling can be particularly helpful in processing emotions and identifying triggers. Writing about daily experiences and feelings can promote self-reflection and help you understand patterns in mood changes.

Furthermore, practicing stress-reduction techniques, such as deep breathing, progressive muscle relaxation, and visualization, can provide immediate relief during overwhelming moments. Identifying personal coping strategies that work for you—whether engaging in hobbies, seeking social support, or spending time in nature—can empower you to navigate the ups and downs of bipolar disorder more effectively

Importance of Routine and Structure

Establishing a daily routine can provide much-needed structure and predictability, which is beneficial for individuals with bipolar disorder. A consistent schedule helps regulate sleep, meals, and activities, reducing the likelihood of triggering mood episodes. Setting small, achievable goals each day can promote a sense of accomplishment and motivation.

Incorporating periods of self-care into your routine is also vital. Designating time for relaxation, hobbies, or socializing helps maintain emotional balance and reduces feelings of isolation. Using planners or apps to organize your daily tasks can aid in creating a structured environment that supports mental health.

Identifying and Managing Triggers

Understanding and managing triggers is a crucial aspect of living with bipolar disorder. Common triggers may include stress, lack of sleep, substance use, or significant life changes. Keeping a journal to document experiences and mood fluctuations can help identify patterns that lead to mood episodes.

Once triggers are identified, developing personalized strategies to manage them is essential. For instance, if stress is a trigger, practicing stress management techniques such as mindfulness or time management can be beneficial. Creating a list of strategies to employ when triggers arise can empower individuals to take proactive steps to maintain emotional stability.

Building Resilience Through Education

Educating yourself about bipolar disorder is an empowering step toward managing the condition effectively. Understanding the nature of the disorder, including its symptoms, causes, and treatment options, can reduce feelings of helplessness and anxiety. Numerous resources, including books, websites, and support groups, can provide valuable information.

Additionally, involving family and friends in the educational process fosters understanding and support. Sharing information about the disorder helps loved ones recognize symptoms and learn how to assist effectively during difficult times. This collective knowledge builds a foundation of empathy and support that is vital for recovery and resilience.

Engaging in Self-Care Practices

Prioritizing self-care is essential for individuals managing bipolar disorder. Activities that promote physical and emotional well-being—such as regular exercise, healthy eating, and adequate sleep—can enhance mood stability. Developing a personalized self-care routine, including practices like meditation, reading, or engaging in creative hobbies, helps foster a positive mindset.

Moreover, regular check-ins with yourself to assess emotional and physical health can prevent the onset of mood swings. Scheduling time for relaxation and activities that bring joy into your life is crucial in maintaining overall well-being. Self-care should be viewed as a non-negotiable part of your routine, allowing for rejuvenation and balance.

Utilizing Professional Support Services

Accessing professional support services is crucial for managing bipolar disorder effectively. This includes not only therapy and medication management but also educational programs and support groups. Finding a qualified mental health professional who specializes in bipolar disorder can provide personalized treatment and guidance tailored to your needs.

In addition to individual therapy, consider group therapy or support groups. These platforms provide valuable connections with others experiencing similar challenges, fostering a sense of community and shared understanding. Engaging with professionals and peers can enhance your coping strategies and provide ongoing support throughout your journey.

CHAPTER 1:

Overview of Bipolar Disorder

History and Evolution of Bipolar Disorder as a Diagnosis

Bipolar disorder has undergone significant changes in its understanding and classification since its earliest descriptions. Initially referred to as "manic-depressive illness," it was first recognized in the 19th century, with prominent figures like Emil Kraepelin contributing to its categorization. Over time, the DSM (Diagnostic and Statistical Manual of Mental Disorders) has refined the diagnostic criteria, reflecting a deeper understanding of the condition's complexity and the spectrum of mood disorders.

In recent decades, research has highlighted the nuanced nature of bipolar disorder, revealing it as a lifelong condition that can manifest in various forms. Today, it is recognized not only as a mood disorder but also in relation to environmental and genetic factors that influence its development and treatment. This evolution in diagnosis aids in more accurate identification and better treatment approaches for those affected.

Prevalence and Demographics: Who Is Affected?

Bipolar disorder affects approximately 1-3% of the global population, with its onset typically occurring in late adolescence or early adulthood. It affects individuals regardless of race, ethnicity, or socioeconomic status, though some studies suggest that there may be slight variations in prevalence among different demographic groups. Understanding these statistics helps to emphasize that bipolar disorder is a common mental health condition, rather than a rare or unusual disorder.

Moreover, both men and women are equally likely to develop bipolar disorder, though the expression of symptoms may differ between genders. Women are more prone to experiencing rapid cycling and depressive episodes, while men often exhibit more manic episodes.

Recognizing these demographic factors can aid in the development of targeted awareness and support initiatives.

Symptoms: Manic, Depressive, and Mixed Episodes

Bipolar disorder is characterized by alternating episodes of mania and depression, which can significantly impact daily functioning. Manic episodes often include elevated mood, increased energy, reduced need for sleep, racing thoughts, and impulsive behavior. During this phase, individuals may feel euphoric and engage in risky activities, making it crucial to recognize these signs for timely intervention.

Conversely, depressive episodes involve feelings of sadness, hopelessness, fatigue, and loss of interest in previously enjoyed activities. Mixed episodes, where symptoms of both mania and depression occur simultaneously, can be particularly challenging, leading to confusion and heightened distress. Understanding these symptoms is essential for recognizing the need for professional help and developing effective coping strategies.

Differences between Bipolar Disorder and Depression

While bipolar disorder and major depressive disorder share some symptoms, they are distinct conditions. The primary difference lies in the presence of manic or hypomanic episodes in bipolar disorder, which are absent in depression. This distinction is vital for accurate diagnosis and treatment, as the management of bipolar disorder often requires mood stabilizers and other medications that differ from those used for unipolar depression.

Additionally, individuals with bipolar disorder experience shifts in mood that can occur over varying periods, whereas those with depression typically maintain a persistently low mood. Recognizing these differences helps individuals seek appropriate care and fosters a better understanding of their mental health challenges.

Co-occurring Disorders and Their Impact

Many individuals with bipolar disorder also experience co-occurring disorders, such as anxiety disorders, substance use disorders, or attention-deficit/hyperactivity disorder (ADHD). These co-existing conditions can complicate diagnosis and treatment, as symptoms may overlap and exacerbate one another. For instance, substance use may temporarily alleviate mood symptoms but ultimately leads to increased instability.

Understanding the impact of co-occurring disorders is essential for creating a comprehensive treatment plan that addresses all aspects of an individual's mental health. Integrated approaches that include therapy, medication, and lifestyle changes can significantly improve overall outcomes and enhance the quality of life for those affected.

Importance of Individualized Treatment Plans

Individualized treatment plans are crucial for effectively managing bipolar disorder, as each person's experience with the illness can vary significantly. Factors such as age, gender, symptoms, personal history, and co-occurring conditions should inform the treatment approach. This tailored strategy can include medication, psychotherapy, lifestyle changes, and coping mechanisms to address specific needs.

Engaging in a collaborative relationship with healthcare providers is essential for developing and adjusting treatment plans as necessary. Regular monitoring and open communication can ensure that the chosen strategies remain effective, promoting stability and enhancing overall mental health.

Myths and Misconceptions about Bipolar Disorder

Numerous myths and misconceptions surround bipolar disorder, often leading to stigma and misunderstanding. One common myth is that bipolar disorder is merely a "mood swing" or personality quirk; in reality, it is a serious mental health condition that requires professional intervention. Such misconceptions can prevent individuals from seeking the help they need and diminish the urgency of addressing their symptoms.

Additionally, another prevalent myth is that individuals with bipolar disorder are inherently dangerous or unpredictable. In fact, most people with bipolar disorder can manage their symptoms effectively with the right support and treatment. Dispelling these myths through education can help reduce stigma and encourage individuals to seek help without fear of judgment.

The Role of Genetics in Bipolar Disorder

Genetics play a significant role in the development of bipolar disorder, with studies indicating that the condition is more common among individuals with a family history of mood disorders. Research has identified several genetic markers that may contribute to the disorder, suggesting that biological factors can predispose individuals to its development. However, having a family history does not guarantee that one will develop the disorder, as environmental factors also play a crucial role.

Understanding the genetic aspect of bipolar disorder can help individuals recognize their risk and the importance of monitoring mental health. It can also foster discussions within families about the need for support, early intervention, and the potential benefits of seeking professional help if symptoms arise.

Environmental Factors Contributing to Bipolar Episodes

Environmental factors, such as stress, trauma, and major life changes, can trigger bipolar episodes in susceptible individuals. Stressful events like losing a job, experiencing a relationship breakup, or facing financial difficulties can act as catalysts for manic or depressive episodes. Recognizing these triggers is essential for managing bipolar disorder effectively.

Implementing stress-reduction techniques, such as mindfulness, exercise, and maintaining a stable routine, can help mitigate the impact of environmental stressors. Developing awareness of personal triggers empowers individuals to create a supportive environment and take proactive steps to manage their mood stability.

Understanding the Brain Chemistry Involved

Bipolar disorder is intricately linked to brain chemistry, particularly neurotransmitters such as serotonin, dopamine, and norepinephrine. Imbalances in these chemicals can lead to the extreme mood swings characteristic of the disorder. Understanding this biochemical basis can demystify the condition and highlight the importance of medication in restoring balance.

Treatment approaches often include mood stabilizers and antidepressants aimed at regulating these neurotransmitters. By working with healthcare providers to find the right medication, individuals can improve their mood stability and overall mental health, making it a key aspect of effective bipolar disorder management.

The Importance of Research and Ongoing Studies

Ongoing research into bipolar disorder is crucial for advancing understanding and treatment options. Studies are exploring various aspects of the disorder, including its causes, effective interventions, and the long-term impact of different treatment modalities. This research contributes to the development of evidence-based practices and helps identify new therapeutic avenues.

Staying informed about the latest findings can empower individuals and families affected by bipolar disorder to advocate for better treatment options and support. Engaging with research through support groups or educational resources can also foster a sense of community and shared understanding.

The Societal Stigma Surrounding Bipolar Disorder

Societal stigma remains a significant barrier for those with bipolar disorder, often leading to discrimination, misunderstanding, and reluctance to seek help. Negative portrayals in media and common misconceptions contribute to this stigma, creating an environment of fear and isolation for affected individuals. Addressing stigma is essential to promote acceptance and encourage individuals to pursue treatment without shame.

Raising awareness and fostering open conversations about bipolar disorder can help challenge these stigmas.

Resources for Further Reading and Support

Numerous resources are available for individuals seeking further information and support regarding bipolar disorder. Organizations such as the National Alliance on Mental Illness (NAMI) and the Depression and Bipolar Support Alliance (DBSA) provide educational materials, support groups, and helplines. These resources can help individuals connect with others who share similar experiences and access valuable information about managing the condition.

Books, online forums, and mental health apps can also offer additional guidance and coping strategies. Utilizing these resources empowers individuals to take an active role in their mental health journey, enhancing their understanding of bipolar disorder and improving their quality of life.

CHAPTER 2:

Diagnosis and Assessment

Importance of Seeking Professional Help

Seeking professional help for bipolar disorder is crucial for accurate diagnosis and effective treatment. Mental health professionals are trained to understand the complexities of mood disorders, which can significantly affect a person's life. They can provide tailored treatment options, including therapy and medication, helping individuals manage their symptoms and improve their quality of life. Reaching out to a professional can also alleviate feelings of isolation, offering a support system during challenging times.

Furthermore, professionals can guide patients through the nuances of the disorder, helping them understand their experiences and how to cope. Early intervention often leads to better outcomes, so it's essential to seek help as soon as possible if symptoms arise. This proactive approach enables individuals to take charge of their mental health and work towards a more stable and fulfilling life.

Types of Mental Health Professionals Involved in Diagnosis

Several types of mental health professionals play key roles in the diagnosis of bipolar disorder. Psychiatrists are medical doctors specializing in mental health who can prescribe medication and conduct in-depth evaluations. Psychologists, often equipped with a doctoral degree, focus on therapy and psychological testing to assess mood disorders. Licensed clinical social workers and licensed professional counselors can also provide therapeutic support and assist in diagnosis.

Choosing the right professional can depend on individual needs and preferences. When seeking help, consider scheduling initial consultations to discuss symptoms and treatment options. This ensures a collaborative approach to diagnosis and treatment, promoting a more effective management plan for bipolar disorder.

Tools and Assessments Used for Diagnosis (e.g., DSM-5 Criteria)

The diagnosis of bipolar disorder often relies on standardized tools and assessments, such as the DSM-5 criteria. This manual outlines specific symptoms and patterns that help mental health professionals determine if an individual meets the criteria for bipolar disorder. The assessment involves evaluating mood episodes, including periods of mania, hypomania, and depression, to establish a clear diagnostic picture.

In addition to the DSM-5, clinicians may use various questionnaires and interviews to gather detailed information about an individual's mood patterns, behavior, and personal history. This systematic approach ensures that the diagnosis is thorough and accurate, leading to more effective treatment options tailored to the individual's needs.

Comprehensive Evaluations: What to Expect

During a comprehensive evaluation for bipolar disorder, expect a detailed assessment of your mental health history and current symptoms. This may involve multiple sessions, during which a mental health professional will ask questions about your mood swings, lifestyle, and any family history of mood disorders. The evaluation might also include standardized tests to assess the severity and frequency of mood episodes.

Additionally, the professional will discuss any co-occurring conditions, such as anxiety or substance use disorders, as these can influence diagnosis and treatment. Understanding what to expect can help reduce anxiety about the process, allowing for a more open and honest dialogue about your mental health.

Self-Assessment Questionnaires and Their Limitations

Self-assessment questionnaires can be helpful tools for individuals to gauge their mental health and identify potential symptoms of bipolar disorder. These questionnaires typically ask about mood fluctuations, energy levels, and behaviors over a specified time. While they can provide insight into one's mental health, it's important to recognize their limitations, as they are not definitive diagnostic tools.

These self-assessments should be seen as a starting point for discussion with a mental health professional rather than a substitute for professional evaluation. Results may vary depending on individual interpretation and self-awareness, so it is crucial to follow up with a trained professional to gain a clearer understanding of any potential mood disorder.

Distinguishing Between Bipolar Disorder and Other Mental Health Issues

Distinguishing bipolar disorder from other mental health issues is essential for appropriate treatment. Symptoms such as mood swings, irritability, and depression can overlap with conditions like major depressive disorder or anxiety disorders. A thorough assessment by a mental health professional is necessary to identify the specific nature of the disorder and tailor treatment accordingly.

To aid in this differentiation, professionals often conduct comprehensive evaluations, including interviews and questionnaires, and consider the patient's history. Understanding the specific characteristics of bipolar disorder, such as the presence of manic or hypomanic episodes, is crucial in arriving at an accurate diagnosis and developing an effective treatment plan.

Role of Family History in Diagnosis

Family history plays a significant role in the diagnosis of bipolar disorder, as genetic factors can influence the likelihood of developing mood disorders. When evaluating a patient, mental health professionals often inquire about any family history of bipolar disorder or other psychiatric conditions. This information can help identify patterns that may indicate a genetic predisposition to the disorder.

Understanding family history not only assists in diagnosis but also informs treatment options. If there is a history of bipolar disorder in the family, healthcare providers may take a more vigilant approach to monitoring symptoms and providing support, enhancing overall management of the condition.

Importance of Accurate Symptom Tracking

Accurate symptom tracking is a vital component of managing bipolar disorder effectively. Keeping a daily record of mood fluctuations, energy levels, and significant life events can help individuals and their healthcare providers identify patterns and triggers. This information is invaluable during consultations, allowing for more informed treatment decisions and adjustments.

To start tracking symptoms, consider using a journal or digital app designed for mental health. Recording feelings and behaviors regularly can provide deeper insights into your mood cycles, leading to better management strategies and enhancing communication with healthcare professionals regarding treatment efficacy.

Understanding the Diagnostic Process Timeline

Understanding the diagnostic process timeline for bipolar disorder can help individuals prepare for what lies ahead. The process typically begins with an initial evaluation, which can last from one to several sessions, depending on the complexity of the case. After this, the healthcare provider may require follow-up assessments and ongoing monitoring to ensure accurate diagnosis and effective treatment.

The timeline can vary significantly based on individual circumstances, including the severity of symptoms and the presence of co-occurring disorders. Being informed about this process can help reduce anxiety and promote a proactive approach to seeking help and adhering to treatment recommendations.

Factors That May Complicate Diagnosis (e.g., Substance Use)

Several factors can complicate the diagnosis of bipolar disorder, with substance use being one of the most significant. Substance abuse can mimic or exacerbate the symptoms of bipolar disorder, making it challenging for healthcare professionals to determine the underlying issue. This overlap can lead to misdiagnosis, resulting in inappropriate or ineffective treatment strategies.

When seeking diagnosis, it's essential to disclose any substance use history to your healthcare provider. This transparency enables a comprehensive evaluation of mood symptoms and ensures that any substance-related issues are addressed alongside mood disorder treatment, leading to better overall outcomes.

Seeking Second Opinions and Advocating for Your Health

If uncertain about a bipolar disorder diagnosis, seeking a second opinion can be a valuable step. Different mental health professionals may offer varying perspectives and insights, which can lead to a more accurate diagnosis or a refined treatment plan. Don't hesitate to ask for a referral to another professional if you feel uncomfortable or unsure about your current care.

Advocating for your health is crucial in the mental health landscape. Prepare for appointments by documenting your symptoms, treatment history, and any concerns you may have. This proactive approach can facilitate better communication with healthcare providers, ensuring your needs are addressed, and that you receive the best possible care.

Support During the Diagnosis Process

Support during the diagnosis process is essential for individuals facing the uncertainty of bipolar disorder. Friends, family, and support groups can provide emotional assistance and practical advice as individuals navigate their mental health journey. Having a trusted support system can alleviate feelings of isolation and anxiety, making the process more manageable.

Additionally, professional support services, such as therapy or counseling, can offer guidance and coping strategies during this challenging time. Connecting with others who have similar experiences can also provide invaluable insights and foster a sense of community, helping individuals feel understood and less alone in their struggles.

Initial Steps Following a Diagnosis

After receiving a diagnosis of bipolar disorder, taking initial steps to manage the condition is critical. Begin by discussing treatment options with your healthcare provider, which may include therapy, medication, or a combination of both. It's essential to establish a treatment plan that suits your needs and to have regular follow-ups to monitor progress.

In addition to professional treatment, incorporating lifestyle changes can significantly impact mood stability. This may involve developing routine, practicing stress-reduction techniques such as mindfulness or yoga, and establishing a support network of friends and family. These steps can enhance overall well-being and improve the effectiveness of professional treatment.

CHAPTER 3:

Treatment Options

Overview of Treatment Modalities: Medication, Therapy, Lifestyle Changes

Bipolar disorder treatment typically involves a combination of medication, psychotherapy, and lifestyle adjustments. Medication can stabilize mood fluctuations, while therapy provides tools to understand and manage emotions. Lifestyle changes, such as maintaining a regular sleep schedule and healthy diet, can significantly impact mood stability and overall well-being.

To effectively address bipolar disorder, it's essential to explore all three modalities in tandem. This holistic approach empowers individuals to manage symptoms and improve their quality of life. Regular check-ins with healthcare providers can help ensure that all aspects of treatment are coordinated and effective.

Types of Medications Commonly Prescribed (e.g., Mood Stabilizers, Antipsychotics)

Medications for bipolar disorder often include mood stabilizers, antipsychotics, and sometimes antidepressants. Mood stabilizers, such as lithium, help to smooth out the highs and lows of mood swings, preventing extreme episodes. Antipsychotics can be useful during manic or psychotic phases to manage symptoms effectively.

When starting medication, it's crucial to work closely with a healthcare provider to find the most effective type and dosage. Individual responses to medication vary, so patience and communication with a healthcare provider are key in determining the right prescription plan.

Understanding the Role of Psychotherapy (e.g., CBT, DBT)

Psychotherapy is a vital component of managing bipolar disorder, offering strategies for coping with mood swings and enhancing emotional resilience. Cognitive Behavioral Therapy (CBT) helps individuals identify and change negative thought patterns, while Dialectical Behavior Therapy (DBT) focuses on emotional regulation and interpersonal effectiveness.

Engaging in regular therapy sessions can provide a supportive space to explore feelings and develop coping mechanisms. These therapeutic approaches empower individuals to navigate the complexities of bipolar disorder and equip them with skills to manage their symptoms effectively.

Importance of Finding the Right Medication Regimen

Finding the right medication regimen is crucial for effective management of bipolar disorder. Each individual may respond differently to medications, making it essential to have an open dialogue with healthcare providers. This process often involves trial and error to determine the best combination of medications.

Regular follow-up appointments are important for assessing medication effectiveness and side effects. Keeping a mood diary can help track changes and patterns, facilitating informed discussions with healthcare providers about necessary adjustments to the treatment plan.

Complementary Therapies: Mindfulness, Yoga, and Exercise

Incorporating complementary therapies such as mindfulness, yoga, and exercise can enhance the management of bipolar disorder. Mindfulness practices foster present-moment awareness, helping individuals reduce anxiety and improve emotional regulation. Yoga offers physical benefits and relaxation techniques that can contribute to overall mental well-being.

Regular physical activity is also essential, as it can boost mood and reduce stress. Finding enjoyable activities encourages consistent engagement, leading to a more balanced lifestyle that supports mental health.

Integrating these practices into daily routines can promote a sense of calm and stability.

Creating a Collaborative Treatment Plan with Healthcare Providers

Developing a collaborative treatment plan with healthcare providers is fundamental for effective management of bipolar disorder. This involves discussing symptoms, treatment options, and preferences to create a personalized plan. Active participation ensures that individuals feel empowered and invested in their recovery journey.

A collaborative approach fosters open communication, making it easier to address concerns and make necessary adjustments. Regular check-ins can reinforce the partnership between patients and providers, ensuring that the treatment plan remains aligned with the individual's needs and goals.

Regular Monitoring and Adjusting Treatment as Needed

Regular monitoring of treatment effectiveness is essential in managing bipolar disorder. Healthcare providers should conduct periodic assessments to evaluate the individual's response to medications and therapies. This ongoing evaluation helps identify any need for adjustments in treatment to better address changing symptoms.

Keeping track of mood fluctuations and side effects in a journal can provide valuable insights for both the patient and healthcare provider. This proactive approach allows for timely interventions and ensures that individuals receive the most appropriate care throughout their journey.

Managing Medication Side Effects

Managing medication side effects is a crucial aspect of bipolar disorder treatment. Many medications can produce unwanted effects that may deter individuals from adhering to their treatment plans. It's important to communicate openly with healthcare providers about any side effects experienced.

Providers may recommend strategies to mitigate side effects, such as adjusting the dosage or switching medications. Lifestyle changes, such as diet and hydration, may also alleviate some side effects. Staying informed and engaged in discussions about medications can empower individuals to manage their treatment effectively.

Importance of Adherence to Prescribed Treatments

Adhering to prescribed treatments is critical for managing bipolar disorder and achieving stability. Skipping medications or therapy sessions can lead to mood swings and exacerbation of symptoms. Establishing a routine can help individuals remember to take medications consistently and attend appointments regularly.

Using tools like pill organizers or reminders can aid in adherence. It's also helpful to discuss any barriers to following the treatment plan with healthcare providers, who can offer solutions or adjustments to make adherence easier.

Understanding the Role of Emergency Interventions

Emergency interventions may be necessary during severe episodes of mania or depression, where safety is at risk. Knowing when to seek immediate help, whether through crisis hotlines or emergency services, is essential for ensuring safety. Individuals should have a clear understanding of their symptoms and what constitutes an emergency.

Creating an emergency contact list, including healthcare providers and supportive family members, can streamline access to help during critical times. Developing this plan ahead of time empowers individuals to act quickly and decisively in a crisis, ensuring that they receive the appropriate care.

Developing a Crisis Management Plan

A crisis management plan is a proactive approach to handling severe mood episodes. This plan should outline specific warning signs, coping strategies, and contacts for support. Collaborating with healthcare providers to create this plan ensures it is comprehensive and tailored to the individual's needs.

Having a written plan can provide clarity and reassurance during times of distress. It serves as a guide for both the individual and their loved ones, helping everyone know how to respond effectively in a crisis situation, minimizing confusion and potential harm.

Engaging Family in Treatment Decisions

Involving family members in treatment decisions can enhance support systems for individuals with bipolar disorder. Family members can provide valuable insights and emotional support while also being educated about the disorder to foster understanding. Engaging them in discussions about treatment plans encourages shared responsibility and accountability.

Regular family meetings with healthcare providers can facilitate communication and ensure everyone is on the same page. This involvement can also help family members recognize warning signs and know how to respond effectively, creating a stronger support network.

Seeking Support from Mental Health Organizations

Mental health organizations can offer resources, education, and support for individuals with bipolar disorder and their families. These organizations often provide access to support groups, educational materials, and workshops to help individuals better understand their condition. Engaging with these resources can empower individuals and reduce feelings of isolation.

Participating in support groups can foster connections with others facing similar challenges, providing a sense of community and shared experience. These organizations can also guide individuals in finding qualified healthcare providers, enhancing the overall treatment experience.

CHAPTER 4:

Coping Mechanisms for Mood Swings

Importance of Developing Coping Strategies

Developing effective coping strategies is crucial for individuals with bipolar disorder, as they provide tools to manage mood swings and navigate emotional highs and lows. These strategies help individuals to respond constructively to challenging situations rather than react impulsively. By creating a personalized coping plan, individuals can identify techniques that resonate with them, which can foster a sense of control over their symptoms.

To implement coping strategies, start by exploring various options, such as mindfulness practices, cognitive-behavioral techniques, and grounding exercises. It's helpful to keep a list of these strategies on hand, so they can be easily accessed during difficult times. Regularly reviewing and updating this plan can ensure that it remains relevant to your evolving needs.

Identifying Personal Triggers and Warning Signs

Recognizing personal triggers and warning signs is essential for managing bipolar disorder. Triggers can be environmental, emotional, or social factors that precipitate mood changes, while warning signs are early indicators that a mood episode may be developing. Keeping a detailed journal of mood fluctuations can help identify patterns, allowing individuals to anticipate potential episodes and take preventive action.

To identify triggers, reflect on past experiences when mood shifts occurred and note any commonalities. This might include specific stressors, changes in routine, or significant life events. Once identified, create a plan to address these triggers, such as avoiding certain situations or developing strategies to cope when facing them.

Techniques for Managing Manic Episodes (e.g., Grounding Exercises)

During manic episodes, individuals may experience heightened energy and impulsivity, making it essential to implement grounding exercises. These techniques help bring focus back to the present moment, reducing overwhelming feelings. Simple grounding methods include engaging the senses—such as describing five things you see, four things you can touch, three things you hear, two things you smell, and one thing you taste.

In addition to grounding exercises, consider establishing a calming routine that incorporates relaxation techniques like deep breathing or yoga. Having a go-to set of strategies for managing mania can help maintain stability and reduce the likelihood of impulsive decisions that could lead to negative consequences.

Strategies for Coping with Depressive Episodes

Coping with depressive episodes often requires a multifaceted approach. First, it is crucial to establish a routine that includes regular sleep, nutrition, and exercise, as these factors can significantly impact mood. Aim for small, achievable goals to foster a sense of accomplishment, even during low periods.

In addition to routine, engage in activities that bring joy or relaxation. This could include hobbies, spending time in nature, or connecting with loved ones. Having a list of enjoyable activities to refer to can provide motivation during depressive phases, encouraging individuals to take small steps toward improving their mood

Role of Routine in Stabilizing Mood

Maintaining a consistent routine plays a vital role in stabilizing mood for individuals with bipolar disorder. A structured daily schedule helps regulate sleep patterns, eating habits, and activity levels, reducing the chances of mood fluctuations. Establishing a routine can also provide a sense of normalcy, making it easier to navigate challenging times.

To create an effective routine, start by setting specific times for waking up, meals, work, and relaxation. Use planners or apps to help track daily tasks and commitments. Incorporating flexibility into the routine allows for adjustments as needed while maintaining the overall structure that supports mental health.

Stress Management Techniques (e.g., Deep Breathing, Meditation)

Effective stress management techniques are essential for individuals with bipolar disorder, as stress can trigger mood episodes. Deep breathing exercises, which involve inhaling deeply through the nose and exhaling slowly through the mouth, can help calm the mind and body. Practicing deep breathing for a few minutes daily can significantly reduce stress levels.

Meditation is another powerful tool for managing stress. Beginners can start with guided meditation apps or videos that provide step-by-step instructions.

Dedicating just a few minutes each day to meditation can enhance mindfulness, promote relaxation, and improve overall emotional well-being.

Importance of Self-Care Practices

Prioritizing self-care is crucial for individuals with bipolar disorder, as it supports overall mental and physical health. Self-care practices can include maintaining a balanced diet, engaging in regular exercise, and ensuring adequate sleep. By nurturing the body, individuals are better equipped to manage the challenges of bipolar disorder.

Incorporate self-care into your daily routine by scheduling time for activities that promote well-being. This might include taking relaxing baths, reading, or practicing hobbies. By treating self-care as a priority, individuals can enhance their resilience and create a more balanced life.

Building a Support Network of Friends and Family

A strong support network of friends and family can significantly impact the well-being of individuals with bipolar disorder. Open communication with trusted loved ones about one's experiences and needs fosters understanding and encouragement. This support system can provide emotional reassurance during challenging times and celebrate achievements during stable periods.

To build this network, consider reaching out to those who have shown support in the past. Be clear about your needs and how they can help, whether through regular check-ins or simply being available to listen. Joining support groups or connecting with others who share similar experiences can also expand your network and provide additional resources.

Utilizing Journaling for Emotional Processing

Journaling serves as a powerful tool for emotional processing, allowing individuals to articulate their thoughts and feelings related to their bipolar disorder. Regularly writing about experiences can clarify emotions and reveal patterns or triggers. This practice can also enhance self-awareness and provide insights into coping strategies that work best.

To begin journaling, set aside a few minutes each day to reflect on your mood, experiences, and any triggers you noticed. Explore not just what you felt but why you might have felt that way. Over time, reviewing past entries can help identify trends and improve emotional regulation.

Understanding the Benefits of Creativity (Art, Music) in Coping

Engaging in creative activities like art and music can provide significant therapeutic benefits for individuals with bipolar disorder. Creativity offers a form of self-expression that can facilitate emotional release, reducing feelings of isolation. Whether painting, playing an instrument, or writing, these activities can serve as healthy outlets for processing emotions.

To incorporate creativity into daily life, set aside time each week to explore artistic pursuits without pressure or judgment. Join community classes, explore online tutorials, or simply dedicate time at home to experiment with different mediums. Embracing creativity can enhance mood and serve as a meaningful coping mechanism.

Developing Resilience through Challenges

Building resilience is an important aspect of managing bipolar disorder, enabling individuals to bounce back from setbacks and navigate challenges effectively. Resilience can be cultivated by adopting a positive mindset, focusing on strengths, and learning from past experiences. Viewing challenges as opportunities for growth can significantly enhance emotional well-being.

To foster resilience, practice reframing negative thoughts into more positive or realistic perspectives. Setting small, achievable goals can also build confidence and reinforce a sense of accomplishment. Over time, these strategies can help develop a stronger emotional foundation to handle the ups and downs of life.

Importance of Patience and Self-Compassion

Practicing patience and self-compassion is essential for individuals managing bipolar disorder. Recovery and stability take time, and it's important to acknowledge that setbacks are a part of the journey. Being kind to oneself during difficult periods can mitigate feelings of guilt or shame, fostering a healthier mindset.

To cultivate self-compassion, treat yourself with the same kindness and understanding that you would offer a friend facing similar struggles. Incorporate affirmations and positive self-talk into your daily routine. This practice can gradually reshape how you view your experiences and enhance overall mental health.

Resources for Further Coping Strategies and Techniques

Exploring additional resources for coping strategies and techniques can empower individuals with bipolar disorder to manage their condition effectively. Numerous books, online courses, and mental health apps provide valuable information on coping mechanisms, self-help strategies, and personal stories. Many mental health organizations also offer resources tailored to those with bipolar disorder.

To find suitable resources, start by researching reputable mental health websites, community centers, or local libraries. Consider seeking recommendations from mental health professionals or support groups. Engaging with these resources can enhance understanding and provide practical strategies for navigating bipolar disorder.

CHAPTER 5:

The Role of Therapy

Overview of Different Therapeutic Approaches

Bipolar disorder can be effectively managed through various therapeutic approaches tailored to individual needs. These therapies include Cognitive Behavioral Therapy (CBT), Dialectical Behavior Therapy (DBT), family therapy, and group therapy. Each method focuses on different aspects of mental health, allowing individuals to gain insights into their condition, develop coping strategies, and foster emotional regulation. Understanding the available therapies empowers individuals to make informed choices about their treatment journey.

Selecting the right therapeutic approach depends on personal preferences, the severity of the disorder, and the presence of supportive relationships. For example, some may benefit from the structured nature of CBT, while others might find group therapy beneficial for shared experiences. Engaging in psychoeducation alongside these therapies helps individuals and their families better comprehend bipolar disorder, facilitating informed discussions with healthcare providers.

Cognitive Behavioral Therapy (CBT) for Bipolar Disorder

Cognitive Behavioral Therapy (CBT) is a widely used therapeutic approach that helps individuals identify and challenge negative thought patterns contributing to mood swings. Through structured sessions, patients learn to replace unhelpful thoughts with more balanced perspectives, reducing the impact of anxiety and depression. The therapy often includes homework assignments, where individuals practice these skills in real-life situations, promoting active engagement in their recovery.

To effectively implement CBT, patients are encouraged to maintain a mood diary, tracking daily emotions and triggers. This practice not only aids therapists in understanding the patient's experience but also empowers individuals to recognize patterns in their moods, leading to proactive coping strategies. Over time, CBT can foster resilience and improve overall emotional regulation, making it a powerful tool for managing bipolar disorder.

Dialectical Behavior Therapy (DBT) and Its Relevance

Dialectical Behavior Therapy (DBT) focuses on enhancing emotional regulation, distress tolerance, and interpersonal effectiveness. Originally developed for individuals with borderline personality disorder, DBT has proven effective for those with bipolar disorder, particularly in managing intense emotions and preventing self-destructive behaviors. The therapy emphasizes mindfulness practices, helping individuals stay present and reduce impulsive reactions during mood swings.

DBT incorporates both individual therapy sessions and skills training groups. In skills training, participants learn techniques such as emotional regulation, interpersonal effectiveness, and distress tolerance. Regular practice of these skills in real-life situations can lead to significant improvements in emotional stability and relationships, making DBT a relevant approach for those seeking comprehensive coping mechanisms for bipolar disorder.

Family Therapy and Its Impact on Recovery

Family therapy involves the participation of family members in the therapeutic process, aiming to improve communication, resolve conflicts, and foster a supportive home environment. This approach recognizes that family dynamics significantly influence the recovery journey of individuals with bipolar disorder. By facilitating open dialogues, family therapy helps family members understand the illness and how to best support their loved one.

To implement family therapy, therapists may use structured sessions where all members can express their thoughts and feelings in a safe space. The therapist may also provide strategies for family members to manage their own emotional responses and encourage healthier interactions. This collaborative approach enhances understanding, reduces stigma within the family, and can significantly impact the recovery and emotional well-being of the person with bipolar disorder.

Group Therapy: Benefits and Support from Peers

Group therapy offers a supportive environment where individuals with bipolar disorder can connect with peers facing similar challenges. These sessions provide a platform for sharing experiences, fostering empathy, and learning from one another's coping strategies. The normalization of shared experiences can reduce feelings of isolation, as participants recognize that they are not alone in their struggles.

In group therapy, a trained facilitator guides discussions, ensuring that all participants have the opportunity to share while maintaining a respectful and safe environment. Activities may include sharing personal stories, discussing triggers, and practicing coping techniques together. This collective support system can enhance motivation and accountability, ultimately contributing to improved mental health outcomes.

Psycho education: Understanding the Illness through Therapy

Psycho education involves educating individuals and their families about bipolar disorder, including its symptoms, treatment options, and coping strategies. This process helps demystify the illness, reducing fear and stigma associated with it. By understanding the biological, psychological, and social factors involved, individuals can engage more meaningfully in their treatment and make informed decisions regarding their care.

To implement psycho education, therapists may provide resources such as informational pamphlets, workshops, or support groups. Family members are encouraged to participate, as their understanding of the illness can enhance their support for the individual. This collaborative approach not only equips individuals with knowledge but also fosters an environment of empathy and support among family and friends.

Integrating Therapy with Medication Management

Integrating therapy with medication management is crucial for effective bipolar disorder treatment. While medications can help stabilize mood, therapy provides essential tools for coping with the emotional and behavioral challenges of the disorder. A coordinated approach ensures that individuals receive holistic care, addressing both the biological and psychological aspects of their condition.

To effectively integrate these approaches, open communication between the therapist and psychiatrist is vital. Regular updates on mood changes and side effects can inform medication adjustments, while therapy sessions can focus on addressing the emotional impact of medication. This synergy between therapy and medication enhances treatment effectiveness, leading to improved overall outcomes.

Finding the Right Therapist for Your Needs

Finding the right therapist involves considering various factors such as expertise in bipolar disorder, therapeutic approach, and personal compatibility. It is essential to seek someone who understands the complexities of the condition and can provide tailored support. Recommendations from healthcare providers, online directories, or support groups can help identify qualified therapists.

During the initial consultations, potential therapists should be asked about their experience with bipolar disorder and their therapeutic techniques. Building a trusting relationship is essential for effective therapy, so individuals should feel comfortable discussing their concerns and preferences. Ultimately, the right therapist can significantly impact the recovery journey, facilitating emotional growth and resilience.

Importance of Therapy Continuity

Continuity in therapy is vital for maintaining progress in managing bipolar disorder. Regular sessions provide ongoing support, allowing individuals to process experiences, track mood changes, and refine coping strategies. Consistency in therapeutic relationships fosters trust, enabling deeper exploration of personal challenges and emotional growth.

To ensure continuity, individuals are encouraged to prioritize their therapy appointments, setting reminders and scheduling sessions in advance. In the event of a missed appointment, contacting the therapist promptly to reschedule can help minimize disruptions in the therapeutic process. By valuing therapy continuity, individuals can sustain their momentum in recovery and enhance their overall mental health.

Addressing Issues of Trust in the Therapeutic Relationship

Trust is a fundamental component of the therapeutic relationship, particularly for individuals managing bipolar disorder. Establishing a trusting environment allows for open communication and vulnerability, essential for effective therapy. Therapists can foster trust by demonstrating empathy, active listening, and non-judgmental support throughout the treatment process.

If trust issues arise, it's important for individuals to address these feelings with their therapist. Open discussions about concerns can lead to deeper understanding and resolution, strengthening the therapeutic alliance. Building a strong rapport enhances the effectiveness of therapy and supports the individual's journey toward emotional stability.

Role of Therapy in Crisis Intervention

Therapy plays a crucial role in crisis intervention for individuals with bipolar disorder. During crises, individuals may experience intense emotions or thoughts that could lead to self-harm or other harmful behaviors. Therapists are trained to recognize signs of a crisis and can provide immediate support and coping strategies to help manage these situations effectively.

In a crisis, therapists may employ techniques such as grounding exercises, emotional regulation skills, and safety planning. Establishing a crisis plan during non-crisis times can also be beneficial, outlining steps to take when overwhelming feelings arise. By equipping individuals with tools for crisis management, therapy can significantly reduce the risk of harm and promote safety during difficult times.

Tracking Progress Through Therapy Sessions

Tracking progress in therapy is essential for evaluating the effectiveness of treatment for bipolar disorder. Keeping a record of feelings, triggers, and coping strategies can provide valuable insights into patterns and improvements over time. This practice allows both the individual and the therapist to assess what is working and what may need adjustment.

Regularly reviewing this progress during therapy sessions encourages active participation in the recovery process. It also reinforces accountability, motivating individuals to engage with their treatment goals. By focusing on progress, therapy can empower individuals to recognize their strengths and resilience, fostering a sense of achievement and hope.

Importance of Setting Goals in Therapy

Setting clear and achievable goals in therapy is crucial for individuals managing bipolar disorder. Goals provide direction and focus, allowing individuals to work towards specific outcomes such as improving emotional regulation or enhancing relationships. Collaboratively developing these goals with a therapist ensures they are personalized and relevant to the individual's unique needs.

To effectively implement goal-setting, individuals should break larger goals into smaller, manageable steps. Regularly reviewing and adjusting these goals in therapy sessions can help maintain motivation and address any barriers encountered along the way. By prioritizing goal-setting, individuals can enhance their sense of agency and progress in their mental health journey.

CHAPTER 6:

Lifestyle Changes and Self-Care

Importance of a Healthy Lifestyle in Managing Bipolar Disorder

A healthy lifestyle plays a crucial role in managing bipolar disorder by promoting overall well-being and stability. Consistent healthy habits can help regulate mood swings, reduce the frequency of episodes, and improve the quality of life. Individuals can achieve this by integrating balanced nutrition, regular exercise, sufficient sleep, and stress management techniques into their daily routines.

To implement a healthy lifestyle, start by assessing your current habits and identifying areas for improvement. Establish specific, achievable goals, such as preparing nutritious meals, exercising for at least 30 minutes a day, or prioritizing sleep hygiene. By making small, incremental changes and maintaining consistency, individuals can experience significant improvements in their mental health.

Nutritional Considerations: Foods That Support Mental Health

Nutrition is a key factor in managing bipolar disorder, as certain foods can positively influence mood and brain function. Incorporating a diet rich in whole foods—such as fruits, vegetables, whole grains, lean proteins, and healthy fats—can provide essential nutrients that support mental health. Omega-3 fatty acids found in fish, nuts, and seeds have been particularly shown to benefit mood stabilization.

To enhance your diet, consider planning meals that include a variety of these nutrient-dense foods. Meal prepping can be an effective strategy to ensure you have healthy options readily available, reducing the likelihood of resorting to unhealthy choices during mood swings. Keeping a food diary can also help you track how certain foods impact your mood and overall well-being.

The Role of Regular Exercise in Mood Stabilization

Regular exercise is a powerful tool for stabilizing mood in individuals with bipolar disorder. Physical activity stimulates the release of endorphins, the body's natural mood lifters, which can help alleviate symptoms of depression and anxiety. Aim for at least 150 minutes of moderate exercise each week, including aerobic activities like walking, swimming, or cycling, along with strength training.

To integrate exercise into your routine, choose activities you enjoy to increase adherence and motivation. Setting specific workout goals, like attending a class or completing a certain number of workouts each week, can also provide structure and accountability. Finding a workout buddy or joining a group can enhance enjoyment and provide social support.

Sleep Hygiene: Establishing Healthy Sleep Patterns

Establishing healthy sleep patterns is essential for managing bipolar disorder, as sleep disturbances can trigger mood episodes. Aim for 7-9 hours of quality sleep each night by maintaining a consistent sleep schedule, going to bed, and waking up at the same time every day. Create a relaxing bedtime routine that may include reading, meditating, or taking a warm bath.

To improve sleep hygiene, consider creating a sleep-friendly environment. Keep your bedroom dark, quiet, and cool, and limit exposure to screens before bedtime. Avoid caffeine and heavy meals close to bedtime, as these can interfere with sleep quality. If you struggle to fall asleep, techniques like deep breathing exercises or progressive muscle relaxation can help calm your mind.

Importance of Mindfulness and Meditation Practices

Mindfulness and meditation practices are effective strategies for managing mood swings associated with bipolar disorder. These techniques can enhance self-awareness, reduce stress, and promote emotional regulation. Start by dedicating a few minutes each day to mindfulness exercises, such as focused breathing, body scans, or guided meditations.

To incorporate mindfulness into your daily life, try integrating it into routine activities, like eating or walking. Practice being present and fully engaged in the moment, noticing thoughts and feelings without judgment. Utilizing apps or attending local classes can also provide guidance and support in establishing a regular mindfulness practice.

Developing a Structured Daily Routine

Creating a structured daily routine can provide stability and predictability for individuals with bipolar disorder. A consistent schedule helps to regulate sleep, meals, activities, and self-care, reducing the likelihood of mood fluctuations. Start by outlining a typical day, including set times for waking, eating, working, and relaxing.

To ensure your routine is manageable and effective, include breaks and time for self-care activities. Flexibility is also important; allow for adjustments when necessary while maintaining core components of your routine. Utilizing planners, reminders, or digital tools can help keep you on track and reinforce the structure in your daily life.

Engaging in Hobbies and Interests for Emotional Well-Being

Participating in hobbies and interests can significantly enhance emotional well-being for individuals managing bipolar disorder. Engaging in activities you enjoy fosters a sense of accomplishment, boosts mood, and provides a positive outlet for expression. Explore various hobbies, such as painting, gardening, writing, or playing music, to discover what resonates with you.

To incorporate hobbies into your routine, set aside dedicated time each week to focus on activities that bring you joy. This can help create a sense of balance in your life and serve as a healthy distraction during challenging times. Additionally, consider joining clubs or groups related to your interests to expand social connections and find support.

Setting Boundaries in Personal and Professional Life

Setting boundaries is vital for maintaining mental health, particularly for individuals with bipolar disorder. Establishing clear limits in personal and professional relationships helps prevent over commitment and reduces stress. Identify areas in your life where boundaries may be necessary, such as work responsibilities or social obligations, and communicate these limits to others assertively.

To practice setting boundaries, start with small steps, such as saying no to extra commitments or scheduling downtime for you. Regularly assess your boundaries and adjust them as needed based on your current mental state. This practice can empower you to prioritize your well-being and maintain a healthier balance in your life.

Avoiding Substance Use and Its Impact on Bipolar Disorder

Avoiding substance use is crucial for individuals with bipolar disorder, as drugs and alcohol can exacerbate symptoms and interfere with treatment. Substance use can destabilize mood, increase the likelihood of episodes, and hinder recovery efforts. Recognizing triggers and seeking healthier coping mechanisms is essential for maintaining mental health.

To avoid substance use, develop strategies for managing stress and emotional discomfort, such as engaging in physical activities or practicing relaxation techniques.

Surround yourself with supportive individuals who respect your commitment to sobriety, and consider seeking professional help if substance use becomes a concern. Joining support groups can also provide a sense of community and accountability.

Importance of Hydration and Its Effects on Mood

Proper hydration is often overlooked but plays a significant role in mood regulation. Dehydration can lead to fatigue, irritability, and difficulty concentrating, which can exacerbate mood swings in individuals with bipolar disorder. Aim to drink at least eight 8-ounce glasses of water daily, adjusting based on activity level and climate.

To maintain hydration, keep a water bottle with you throughout the day as a reminder to drink regularly. Consider incorporating hydrating foods into your diet, such as fruits and vegetables, to boost your fluid intake. Monitoring urine color can also serve as a simple indicator of hydration status—aim for light yellow as a sign of adequate hydration.

Maintaining Social Connections and Relationships

Maintaining social connections is vital for emotional support and well-being in individuals with bipolar disorder. Healthy relationships can provide comfort, understanding, and a sense of belonging. Make a conscious effort to nurture existing relationships and reach out to friends or family regularly, even during difficult times.

To strengthen your social connections, schedule regular check-ins or social activities with loved ones. Joining support groups or community organizations can also help you meet new people who share similar experiences. Building a strong support network enhances resilience and can provide valuable resources for coping with mood fluctuations.

Creating a Personal Self-Care Plan

Developing a personal self-care plan is essential for managing bipolar disorder effectively. A self-care plan should outline strategies and activities that promote mental, emotional, and physical well-being. Begin by identifying specific self-care activities that resonate with you, such as meditation, exercise, or engaging in hobbies.

To implement your self-care plan, set aside time each week to prioritize these activities. Keep track of your progress and adjust the plan as necessary to meet your evolving needs. Consistent self-care practices can serve as a buffer against stress and help maintain emotional stability.

Resources for Healthy Lifestyle Changes

Numerous resources are available to support individuals in making healthy lifestyle changes to manage bipolar disorder effectively. Books, online courses, and mental health apps can provide valuable information and guidance. Additionally, seeking the assistance of a registered dietitian or mental health professional can offer personalized strategies tailored to your needs.

To access these resources, consider exploring reputable websites dedicated to mental health, local community centers, or wellness programs. Many organizations also offer workshops or support groups focused on lifestyle changes. Taking advantage of these resources can empower you to make informed choices and enhance your overall well-being.

CHAPTER 7:

Managing Relationships

The Impact of Bipolar Disorder on Personal Relationships

Bipolar disorder can significantly affect personal relationships due to the mood swings associated with the condition. When experiencing mania or depression, individuals may exhibit behaviors that can strain their connections with friends, family, and partners. For instance, during manic episodes, one might be overly energetic and impulsive, leading to misunderstandings and conflicts. Conversely, depressive phases can cause withdrawal, making it challenging to maintain intimacy and engagement.

To mitigate these impacts, it's essential for individuals with bipolar disorder to communicate openly about their condition with those close to them. Transparency can foster understanding and patience, helping loved ones recognize that the behavior is part of the illness rather than a reflection of their feelings toward them. Developing strategies to manage these mood fluctuations can strengthen bonds and create a supportive environment.

Communication Strategies with Loved Ones

Effective communication is vital for navigating the complexities of relationships affected by bipolar disorder. Individuals should aim for clarity and honesty when discussing their feelings and experiences. Utilizing "I" statements, such as "I feel overwhelmed when..." can help express emotions without placing blame on others, facilitating a more constructive dialogue.

Additionally, establishing regular check-ins with loved ones can foster ongoing communication. These discussions can be structured, where both parties share their feelings and thoughts in a safe space, ensuring that concerns are addressed before they escalate. Encouraging open dialogue can help maintain a supportive atmosphere and reduce the likelihood of misunderstandings.

Educating Family and Friends about Bipolar Disorder

Educating family and friends about bipolar disorder is crucial for fostering understanding and empathy. Sharing reliable resources, such as articles, videos, or books, can help loved ones grasp the nature of the disorder, its symptoms, and the challenges faced by those living with it. Consider organizing a casual discussion or information session to explain how bipolar disorder manifests and what they can expect during various episodes.

Moreover, it's beneficial to share personal experiences and how they relate to the disorder. This approach helps to humanize the condition and reinforces the message that the person is not defined by their illness. Creating an informed support network can lead to more compassionate interactions and a greater willingness to assist when challenges arise.

Setting Boundaries with Friends and Family

Setting clear boundaries is essential for maintaining healthy relationships when managing bipolar disorder. Individuals should communicate their needs, such as the importance of space during depressive episodes or the necessity for support during manic phases. Establishing these limits helps prevent misunderstandings and ensures that both parties know what to expect from one another.

To implement boundaries effectively, it may be helpful to have open discussions with loved ones about what is comfortable and what is not. This process should involve active listening and collaboration, allowing everyone to express their concerns and preferences. By respecting each other's boundaries, relationships can thrive while minimizing the potential for conflict and emotional distress.

Importance of Understanding Partner Dynamics

Understanding partner dynamics is critical for individuals with bipolar disorder and their significant others. Each partner's coping mechanisms and emotional responses can differ, which may affect how they interact during mood fluctuations. Acknowledging these differences allows for a more empathetic approach to handling situations, promoting a healthier partnership.

Couples may benefit from discussing their unique perspectives on bipolar disorder and how it influences their relationship. Engaging in couples therapy can provide a neutral space to explore these dynamics, offering tools to enhance communication and conflict resolution. By working together, partners can develop a deeper understanding of one another and strengthen their emotional bond.

Managing Conflicts and Disagreements Constructively

Managing conflicts and disagreements constructively is vital for sustaining relationships impacted by bipolar disorder. When emotions run high, taking a step back to cool off can be beneficial. Agreeing on a "cooling-off" period allows both parties to process their feelings before reconvening to discuss the issue at hand.

Additionally, practicing active listening during discussions can foster understanding. Each person should strive to express their viewpoints without interrupting the other, ensuring both sides feel heard. Utilizing conflict resolution strategies, such as finding common ground or brainstorming solutions together, can lead to more productive outcomes and reinforce the relationship.

The Role of Support Groups in Fostering Relationships

Support groups play a significant role in fostering relationships for individuals with bipolar disorder. By connecting with others who share similar experiences, individuals can gain insights and learn coping strategies that can be applied within their personal relationships. These groups often provide a safe environment for sharing feelings and challenges, reducing feelings of isolation.

Encouraging loved ones to attend support group sessions can also help them better understand the experiences of individuals with bipolar disorder. This shared knowledge can promote empathy and patience in relationships, allowing family and friends to support their loved one more effectively. Regular participation in support groups can enhance overall relational dynamics and emotional well-being.

Discussing Mental Health with Employers or Colleagues

Discussing mental health with employers or colleagues can be daunting but is often necessary for creating a supportive work environment. Individuals with bipolar disorder should consider disclosing their condition if it impacts their work performance or requires accommodations. Preparing for this conversation by identifying specific needs or adjustments can help facilitate a productive discussion.

Employers often appreciate transparency and may offer resources or flexibility to support employees. It can be beneficial to focus on how the condition affects work, rather than detailing personal struggles. Framing the discussion around finding solutions that enhance productivity can create a more favorable outcome, fostering a supportive atmosphere at work.

Strategies for Involving Loved Ones in the Treatment Process

Involving loved ones in the treatment process can enhance support for individuals managing bipolar disorder. Open communication about treatment goals, therapy sessions, and medication plans helps loved ones understand how to provide effective support. Additionally, inviting them to attend therapy sessions or treatment discussions can create a shared sense of involvement and commitment.

Establishing regular family meetings to discuss progress and challenges can also keep everyone informed and engaged. This collaborative approach helps to reinforce accountability and can lead to a more supportive environment for managing the condition. It allows loved ones to provide encouragement and assistance in ways that align with the individual's treatment plan.

Importance of Maintaining Social Activities

Maintaining social activities is vital for individuals with bipolar disorder, as it fosters connection and a sense of belonging. Engaging in regular social interactions can combat feelings of isolation, which often exacerbate mood swings. Individuals should prioritize scheduling time with friends and participating in group activities that promote positive engagement and enjoyment.

Creating a balanced social calendar that accommodates personal needs is crucial. This approach may involve setting limits on how often to participate in social events, ensuring there is adequate time for rest and self-care. By nurturing social connections, individuals can enhance their emotional well-being and resilience in managing bipolar disorder.

Handling Isolation and Its Effects on Mood

Handling isolation effectively is essential for mitigating its negative effects on mood for individuals with bipolar disorder. Recognizing the signs of withdrawal and consciously seeking social interactions can help break the cycle of isolation. Engaging in simple activities, such as texting a friend or joining an online community, can initiate reconnection and support.

Establishing routines that include social engagement can also counteract isolation. Scheduling regular meet-ups, joining clubs, or participating in group hobbies can foster connections and maintain mental health. By actively combating isolation, individuals can enhance their mood stability and overall well-being.

Rebuilding Relationships After Episodes

Rebuilding relationships after episodes of bipolar disorder requires patience and understanding. It's important to acknowledge any hurtful actions that may have occurred during mood swings and take responsibility. Initiating conversations with loved ones to express remorse and clarify intentions can help mend emotional wounds.

Moving forward, individuals should focus on demonstrating positive changes through their behavior. Consistently showing commitment to treatment and open communication can rebuild trust over time. Re-establishing connections takes effort, but with persistence and sincerity, relationships can emerge stronger and more resilient.

Resources for Relationship Management and Support

Accessing resources for relationship management and support is crucial for individuals with bipolar disorder. Online platforms, hotlines, and local support groups offer valuable information and community. Websites dedicated to mental health can provide articles, forums, and tips on navigating relationships while managing bipolar disorder.

In addition to digital resources, seeking professional guidance from therapists specializing in bipolar disorder can be beneficial. Therapy can offer personalized strategies and coping mechanisms tailored to individual situations. By leveraging available resources, individuals can enhance their relational skills and overall emotional health.

CHAPTER 8:

Handling Crises and Relapses

Understanding the Signs of a Potential Crisis

Recognizing the early signs of a potential crisis in bipolar disorder is crucial for timely intervention. Symptoms may include drastic mood swings, increased irritability, sleep disturbances, and withdrawal from social activities. Monitoring these changes can help individuals and their loved ones identify when a crisis may be imminent, allowing for proactive measures to be taken.

To effectively recognize these signs, individuals can maintain a mood diary to track fluctuations in their emotional state, energy levels, and behaviors. This practice helps in spotting patterns that may precede a crisis, empowering individuals to communicate their needs to family and healthcare providers before the situation escalates.

Developing a Personalized Crisis Management Plan

Creating a personalized crisis management plan is essential for effectively navigating potential crises. This plan should outline specific steps to take when symptoms intensify, including coping strategies, emergency contacts, and a list of resources. Involving a mental health professional in developing this plan can ensure it is comprehensive and tailored to individual needs.

Once the plan is established, it is important to share it with trusted family members or friends. This collaborative approach ensures that those close to the individual are aware of the plan and can provide support during a crisis, making the response to symptoms more effective and coordinated.

Importance of Immediate Support during Crises

Immediate support during a crisis can significantly impact the outcome for individuals experiencing severe mood episodes. This support can come from family, friends, or mental health professionals and may include offering emotional reassurance, assisting with practical tasks, or simply being present. Providing a safe space can help individuals feel understood and less isolated during distressing times.

For optimal effectiveness, those providing support should be aware of the individual's specific needs and preferences during a crisis. Engaging in open communication and active listening can foster a supportive environment, enabling individuals to express their feelings and concerns without fear of judgment.

Strategies for Family Involvement during Relapses

Family involvement during relapses is critical for the recovery process. Open communication about the individual's experiences and feelings can help family members understand the situation better and respond with compassion. Encouraging family members to participate in therapy sessions or educational workshops can also enhance their understanding of bipolar disorder and improve their ability to provide support.

Additionally, establishing clear boundaries and responsibilities can help family members navigate their roles during a relapse. Creating a family support system that includes regular check-ins and open dialogue about emotional well-being can reinforce a collaborative approach to managing bipolar disorder.

The Role of Emergency Services and Hospitalization

In some cases, an individual experiencing a severe bipolar episode may require emergency services or hospitalization. Understanding when to seek help is vital; indicators include suicidal thoughts, extreme mood swings, or the inability to care for oneself. Emergency services can provide immediate support and facilitate necessary interventions, including hospitalization if required.

Hospitalization offers a structured environment where individuals can receive intensive treatment and monitoring. This process often includes medication management, therapy, and the development of a safety plan, ensuring individuals are stable before transitioning back to everyday life.

Techniques for De-escalating Tense Situations

De-escalating tense situations during a crisis involves employing specific techniques to reduce anxiety and restore calm. One effective method is active listening, which entails acknowledging the individual's feelings without judgment. Validating their emotions can help them feel heard and understood, reducing agitation and tension.

In addition to listening, employing calming strategies such as deep breathing exercises or guided imagery can help shift the focus away from distressing thoughts. Encouraging individuals to engage in a grounding technique, like focusing on their surroundings or identifying sensory details, can also help them regain a sense of control and calmness.

Identifying and Addressing the Underlying Causes of Relapses

Identifying underlying causes of relapses is critical for effective management of bipolar disorder. Common triggers may include significant life stressors, changes in routine, or medication noncompliance. Keeping a detailed record of mood changes alongside life events can help pinpoint specific triggers, facilitating proactive interventions in the future.

Once triggers are identified, individuals can work with their mental health professionals to develop strategies to address these causes. This may involve adjusting medication, learning stress management techniques, or establishing a more consistent routine to reduce vulnerability to future relapses.

Importance of Post-Crisis Evaluation and Learning

Post-crisis evaluation is a key component of effective bipolar disorder management. After a crisis, reflecting on the events that occurred can provide valuable insights into what worked, what didn't, and how future situations might be handled differently. Keeping a journal or discussing experiences with a therapist can aid in this evaluation process.

Learning from each crisis allows individuals to refine their crisis management plans and strategies over time. This proactive approach not only enhances resilience but also empowers individuals to feel more in control of their mental health journey.

Re-establishing Routine after a Crisis

Re-establishing routine after a crisis is essential for restoring stability and promoting mental well-being. Start by gradually reintroducing daily activities and schedules that were disrupted during the crisis. This could include regular sleep patterns, meal times, and engaging in hobbies or social activities.

To facilitate this process, individuals can set small, achievable goals that help rebuild a sense of normalcy.

By focusing on routine and structure, individuals can regain a sense of control and predictability, which is vital for overall mental health.

Strategies for Preventing Future Relapses

Preventing future relapses involves a multifaceted approach that includes ongoing self-care, medication adherence, and regular mental health check-ins. Establishing a solid support network and actively participating in therapy can also help individuals recognize early signs of mood changes and take preventive measures.

Additionally, lifestyle factors such as regular exercise, a balanced diet, and sufficient sleep play a crucial role in maintaining mental health stability. Incorporating these habits into daily life can enhance overall well-being and reduce the likelihood of future crises.

Engaging in Follow-Up Care and Monitoring

Engaging in follow-up care is vital for maintaining mental health after a crisis. This includes regular appointments with mental health professionals, where individuals can discuss their progress, any emerging symptoms, and necessary adjustments to their treatment plans. Consistent monitoring allows for early intervention, should any warning signs arise.

Follow-up care can also encompass ongoing support groups or therapy sessions that promote connection with others facing similar challenges. This communal approach fosters understanding and shared experiences, providing individuals with additional resources for managing their condition effectively.

Role of Peer Support During Crises

Peer support plays a significant role during crises by providing individuals with a sense of understanding and community. Connecting with others who have experienced similar challenges can foster empathy and reduce feelings of isolation. Peer support groups can offer valuable insights and coping strategies based on real-life experiences, making them a vital resource during difficult times.

To enhance the effectiveness of peer support, individuals can seek out groups that focus on shared experiences related to bipolar disorder. This connection not only reinforces feelings of belonging but also promotes recovery through mutual support and encouragement.

Resources for Crisis Management Support

Utilizing resources for crisis management support can significantly enhance an individual's ability to navigate bipolar disorder challenges. This may include local mental health hotlines, support groups, or online forums where individuals can seek advice and share experiences. Knowing where to turn for help can provide reassurance and guidance during crises.

Additionally, mental health professionals can recommend specific resources tailored to individual needs, such as therapy options, educational materials, or crisis intervention services. By proactively engaging with these resources, individuals can strengthen their support networks and improve their overall mental health management.

Chapter 9:

Moving Forward: Long-Term Management

Setting Realistic Goals for Long-Term Management

Establishing realistic goals is crucial for managing bipolar disorder effectively. Begin by identifying specific, measurable, achievable, relevant, and time-bound (SMART) goals that focus on different aspects of life, such as personal growth, relationships, or mental health. For instance, instead of aiming for total stability, set a goal to maintain a consistent sleep schedule or practice mindfulness three times a week. This approach helps create a sense of accomplishment and progress.

To achieve these goals, break them down into smaller, manageable steps. Use tools like planners or digital apps to track your progress and adjust your goals as necessary. Regularly review these goals with a mental health professional or support group to stay accountable and motivated, reinforcing the importance of each small victory along the way.

Importance of Ongoing Education About Bipolar Disorder

Understanding bipolar disorder is essential for effective management. Invest time in learning about the symptoms, triggers, and treatments associated with the condition. Utilize reliable resources such as books, reputable websites, and workshops to gain insights into how bipolar disorder affects mood and behavior. This knowledge empowers individuals to recognize early warning signs and respond appropriately.

Engaging in ongoing education can also help demystify misconceptions surrounding the disorder. Consider joining support groups or community classes focused on bipolar disorder to share experiences and gather practical strategies from others facing similar challenges. Continuous learning fosters resilience and enables better coping mechanisms as you navigate the ups and downs of the condition.

Strategies for Maintaining a Positive Outlook

Maintaining a positive outlook can significantly influence mood stability in individuals with bipolar disorder. Incorporate daily practices such as gratitude journaling, where you note three things you appreciate each day, fostering a mindset shift towards positivity. Mindfulness and meditation techniques can also help ground you in the present, reducing anxiety and promoting emotional balance.

Surround yourself with positive influences by cultivating supportive relationships. Engage with friends and family who uplift you and participate in activities that bring joy and fulfillment. By actively choosing to focus on positive experiences and connections, you create a buffer against the mood swings associated with bipolar disorder.

Regular Health Check-Ups and Monitoring

Regular health check-ups are vital for managing bipolar disorder effectively. Schedule consistent appointments with your healthcare provider to monitor your mental and physical health. These check-ups can help detect any early signs of mood swings or side effects from medication, allowing for timely adjustments to your treatment plan.

Keep a health journal to track symptoms, medication responses, and lifestyle factors such as sleep and diet. This documentation can be shared with your doctor to facilitate discussions about your progress and any necessary changes. Staying proactive in your health care helps ensure better management of the disorder over time.

Building Resilience and Adaptability in Life

Resilience is the ability to bounce back from setbacks, which is especially important for individuals with bipolar disorder. Develop resilience by practicing problem-solving skills and maintaining a flexible mindset. When faced with challenges, focus on what you can control and take actionable steps to address the situation, rather than feeling overwhelmed.

Incorporate stress-reducing techniques into your routine, such as regular exercise, hobbies, or relaxation methods. These activities not only improve mood but also enhance adaptability by teaching coping strategies for dealing with unexpected changes in life. By nurturing resilience, you can better navigate the fluctuations of bipolar disorder.

Celebrating Progress and Personal Achievements

Acknowledging and celebrating progress is essential for building self-esteem and motivation. Regularly reflect on your achievements, no matter how small, and reward yourself for reaching milestones in your management journey. This could be as simple as treating yourself to a favorite activity or sharing your accomplishments with loved ones.

Create a visual representation of your progress, such as a progress chart or a vision board. This tangible reminder of your journey can serve as encouragement during tougher times. Celebrating achievements reinforces a sense of agency and purpose, fostering a more positive outlook on your mental health journey.

Importance of Community Involvement and Support

Community involvement plays a crucial role in managing bipolar disorder. Engage in local support groups or mental health organizations that foster connection with others who understand your experiences. These groups provide a safe space for sharing struggles and successes, which can help reduce feelings of isolation.

Volunteering or participating in community events can also boost your mood and sense of belonging. Find opportunities that resonate with your interests, allowing you to contribute meaningfully while connecting with others. Building a strong support network is essential for maintaining mental health and navigating the challenges of bipolar disorder.

Engaging in Advocacy for Mental Health Awareness

Advocacy is a powerful tool for promoting mental health awareness and reducing stigma surrounding bipolar disorder. Start by educating others about the condition and sharing your experiences, whether through social media, blogs, or community events. This not only empowers you but also helps others understand the realities of living with bipolar disorder.

Consider joining or forming advocacy groups that focus on mental health issues. Engage in campaigns, write letters to policymakers, or participate in awareness events. By actively promoting mental health advocacy, you contribute to a larger movement that supports individuals affected by bipolar disorder and fosters a more understanding society.

Developing a Personal Recovery Roadmap

Creating a personal recovery roadmap helps individuals with bipolar disorder outline their goals and strategies for managing the condition. Begin by assessing your current situation, identifying strengths, challenges, and resources available to you. This assessment will provide clarity on the areas you wish to focus on for improvement.

Next, define specific recovery goals, such as enhancing coping skills, establishing a routine, or improving relationships. Break these goals into actionable steps and establish timelines for achieving them. Regularly review and update your roadmap to reflect changes in your circumstances, ensuring it remains relevant and motivating throughout your recovery journey.

The Role of Continued Therapy in Long-Term Management

Ongoing therapy is a cornerstone of effective bipolar disorder management. Regular sessions with a licensed therapist can provide support, insight, and coping strategies tailored to your needs. Cognitive Behavioral Therapy (CBT) is particularly effective for addressing negative thought patterns and developing practical coping skills.

Consider integrating various therapeutic approaches, such as group therapy or art therapy, to explore different facets of your mental health. Staying committed to therapy allows for continuous learning and adjustment of coping strategies, ultimately leading to more effective long-term management of the disorder.

Finding Purpose and Meaning Beyond the Diagnosis

Discovering purpose beyond the bipolar diagnosis can greatly enhance overall well-being. Reflect on your interests, passions, and values to identify activities that provide fulfillment and meaning. Engaging in hobbies, pursuing education, or volunteering can help cultivate a sense of identity that extends beyond the condition.

Additionally, setting personal goals that align with your values reinforces your sense of purpose. Share your journey with others, whether through storytelling or mentoring, as this not only enriches your life but also inspires others facing similar challenges. By focusing on what brings joy and meaning, you can foster a more positive outlook on your mental health journey.

Maintaining a Balanced Life Through Proactive Strategies

Achieving balance in life is essential for managing bipolar disorder effectively. Implement proactive strategies such as creating a structured daily routine that includes time for work, leisure, and self-care. Prioritize activities that promote physical health, such as regular exercise, balanced nutrition, and sufficient sleep.

Limit exposure to stressors by setting boundaries in your personal and professional life. Engage in relaxation techniques like yoga or meditation to help maintain emotional stability. By actively managing your lifestyle, you can create a supportive environment that contributes to balanced mental health and well-being.

Common Concerns

How to Discuss Bipolar Disorder with Loved Ones?

When discussing bipolar disorder with loved ones, start by choosing a calm and private setting where everyone feels comfortable. Use clear, straightforward language to explain what bipolar disorder is, emphasizing that it's a mental health condition, not a character flaw. Share your experiences, including how it affects your daily life, and encourage questions to foster understanding. This approach helps reduce stigma and promotes empathy among your loved ones.

It's also essential to express your needs clearly. Let your loved ones know how they can support you during both manic and depressive episodes. Encourage them to be open about their feelings and concerns, and reassure them that it's okay to ask for clarification on any aspect of your condition. Engaging in ongoing conversations can help strengthen your relationships and build a support network.

What Should I Do If I Experience Side Effects from Medication?

If you experience side effects from your medication, the first step is to keep a detailed record of the symptoms, including their duration and intensity. This information will be invaluable when you discuss the issue with your healthcare provider. Do not stop taking your medication abruptly, as this can worsen your condition. Instead, communicate openly about your experiences, and be prepared to explore alternative treatments or adjustments to your current regimen.

Your doctor may suggest dosage adjustments or switching to a different medication that might better suit your needs. Always follow their guidance and never hesitate to reach out if side effects persist or worsen. Establishing a good rapport with your healthcare provider can make the process of finding the right medication much smoother.

How Can I Support a Friend or Family Member with Bipolar Disorder?

Supporting a friend or family member with bipolar disorder involves educating yourself about the condition to better understand what they are going through. Be patient and listen without judgment when they share their feelings or experiences. Offer to accompany them to therapy sessions or support groups if they are comfortable with that, as this can help them feel less isolated and more supported in their journey.

Encourage healthy habits by engaging in activities that promote mental well-being, such as exercising together, practicing mindfulness, or enjoying hobbies. Check in regularly to show that you care and are available to listen. Be sure to set healthy boundaries for yourself, as supporting someone with bipolar disorder can be emotionally taxing. Prioritizing your mental health ensures that you can provide meaningful support.

What Should I Do If I Feel a Manic or Depressive Episode Coming On?

If you sense a manic or depressive episode approaching, implement your personalized coping strategies immediately. This may include using a mood tracker to identify early warning signs and triggers. Establish a routine that includes regular sleep patterns, balanced meals, and physical activity to help maintain stability. Inform your support network about your warning signs, so they can assist you if needed.

Consider employing grounding techniques, such as mindfulness meditation, deep breathing exercises, or engaging in a calming activity like reading or art. These practices can help redirect your energy and stabilize your mood. If the symptoms worsen, don't hesitate to reach out to your mental health professional for additional support or adjustments to your treatment plan.

How Can I Differentiate Between Normal Mood Swings and Bipolar Disorder Symptoms?

To distinguish between normal mood swings and bipolar disorder symptoms, consider the intensity, duration, and frequency of the mood changes. Normal mood swings are typically short-lived and situational, while bipolar disorder involves extreme mood fluctuations that last for days, weeks, or even months. Look for patterns in your mood changes and any associated changes in behavior, such as shifts in energy levels, sleep patterns, or motivation.

Keeping a journal can be an effective way to monitor your moods over time. Note the circumstances surrounding each mood change and evaluate whether they align with the diagnostic criteria for bipolar disorder. If you suspect that your symptoms may be more than typical mood swings, consult with a mental health professional for a comprehensive assessment.

Frequently Asked Questions (FAQs)

What is the Difference Between Bipolar Disorder I and II?

Bipolar disorder I is characterized by at least one manic episode, which may be preceded or followed by hypomanic or depressive episodes. The manic episodes in bipolar I can be severe and often lead to significant impairment in daily functioning. Conversely, bipolar disorder II involves at least one major depressive episode and at least one hypomanic episode, but it does not include full-blown manic episodes.

Understanding these distinctions can help individuals identify their symptoms more accurately and seek appropriate treatment. If you are uncertain about which type you may be experiencing, discussing your symptoms with a mental health professional is crucial for obtaining a correct diagnosis and tailored treatment plan.

How is Bipolar Disorder Diagnosed?

Bipolar disorder is diagnosed through a comprehensive evaluation conducted by a mental health professional, often including a detailed clinical interview. This process typically involves discussing your symptoms, family history of mental health issues, and any previous episodes of mood disturbances. Questionnaires or mood charts may be used to gather additional information about your mood patterns over time.

It's important to be honest and thorough during the assessment process. Your mental health provider may also rule out other conditions that could cause similar symptoms, such as anxiety disorders or thyroid issues. A correct diagnosis is essential for developing an effective treatment strategy tailored to your needs.

Can Bipolar Disorder Be Cured?

Currently, bipolar disorder cannot be cured, but it can be effectively managed with a combination of medication, therapy, and lifestyle adjustments. Many individuals with bipolar disorder lead fulfilling lives by adhering to their treatment plans and implementing coping strategies. The focus of treatment is on stabilizing mood swings and minimizing the impact of the disorder on daily life.

Engaging in therapy, such as cognitive-behavioral therapy (CBT), can help individuals develop practical skills to manage their symptoms and improve their quality of life. Regular follow-ups with healthcare professionals are also essential to adjust treatment plans as needed, ensuring ongoing support and stability.

How Do I Find a Mental Health Professional?

To find a mental health professional, start by seeking referrals from your primary care doctor, friends, or family. Research potential providers using online directories or mental health organizations, paying attention to their specialties and patient reviews. Consider factors like their treatment approach, experience with bipolar disorder, and whether they accept your insurance.

Once you've identified potential candidates, schedule an initial consultation to gauge whether you feel comfortable with their approach and expertise. It's essential to find a mental health professional who understands your needs and can provide the necessary support throughout your journey.

What Can I Do to Help Manage My Symptoms Daily?

Managing bipolar disorder symptoms daily involves establishing a structured routine that promotes stability. Prioritize sleep by maintaining a consistent sleep schedule, as adequate rest is crucial for mood regulation. Incorporate regular physical activity, balanced nutrition, and mindfulness practices like meditation or yoga into your daily life to enhance overall well-being.

Additionally, keep a mood journal to track your emotional fluctuations, identify triggers, and develop strategies for managing them. Building a support network of friends, family, and mental health professionals can provide valuable encouragement and assistance in your daily management efforts. Regular check-ins with your therapist or support group can reinforce your coping strategies and keep you accountable.

Conclusion

Summary of Key Insights and Strategies for Managing Bipolar Disorder

Understanding the key insights and strategies for managing bipolar disorder is essential for effective self-care. This involves recognizing the symptoms and triggers of mood swings, which can help individuals anticipate and mitigate episodes. Developing a personalized plan that includes medication adherence, therapy, and lifestyle changes—such as regular exercise, healthy eating, and adequate sleep—can significantly improve mood stability.

Implementing daily routines and monitoring mood patterns can also aid in managing the disorder. Keeping a mood journal or using smartphone apps designed for mood tracking allows individuals to identify early warning signs of mood shifts and adjust their coping strategies accordingly. Regular check-ins with a mental health professional can ensure that the management plan remains effective and relevant.

Importance of a Supportive Network and Ongoing Education

Having a supportive network is crucial for individuals living with bipolar disorder. This network can include family, friends, and support groups, all of which play a vital role in providing emotional support and practical assistance during challenging times. Engaging in open communication about the disorder helps reduce stigma and fosters understanding, which can empower both the individual and their loved ones.

Ongoing education about bipolar disorder is equally important. This can be achieved through attending workshops, reading credible resources, and participating in support groups. The more knowledge individuals and their support networks have about the condition, the better equipped they will be to handle its challenges, thus promoting a more supportive and informed environment.

Encouragement for Those Affected to Seek Help and Stay Informed

It's crucial for individuals affected by bipolar disorder to seek help and not hesitate to access mental health services. Professional treatment options, including therapy and medication, can significantly improve quality of life. Encouraging those affected to establish a trusting relationship with a mental health provider fosters a sense of safety and support, making it easier to discuss symptoms and treatment options.

Staying informed about the latest research, treatment options, and coping strategies is also vital for effective management. Utilizing resources such as mental health organizations, online forums, and educational materials can empower individuals to take an active role in their recovery. Regularly engaging with these resources ensures that those affected can make informed decisions about their health and well-being.